Why do cats purr?

Jinny Johnson

Miles Kelly

First published in 2011 by Miles Kelly Publishing Ltd
Harding's Barn, Bardfield End Green, Thaxted,
Essex, CM6 3PX, UK

2 4 6 8 10 9 7 5 3 1

Publishing Director Belinda Gallagher
Creative Director Jo Cowan
Editorial Director Rosie McGuire
Editor Carly Blake
Volume Designer Greg Best
Cover Designer Kayleigh Allen
Image Manager Liberty Newton
Indexer Gill Lee
Production Manager Elizabeth Collins
Reprographics Anthony Cambray, Stephan Davis

ISBN 978-1-84810-453-2

Printed in China

British Library Cataloguing-in-Publication Data

A catalogue record for this book is
available from the British Library

ACKNOWLEDGEMENTS
The publishers would like to thank the following
artist who has contributed to this book:
Mike Foster (character cartoons)
All other artwork from the Miles Kelly Artwork Bank

The publishers would like to thank the following
sources for the use of their photographs:
Dreamstime.com 28 Cvrgrl
Fotolia.com 5 Willee Cole; 9 Fragles;
13 iChip; 24 Mr Flibble
iStockphoto.com 21 Tony Campbell;
26–27 Vladimir Suponev
Shutterstock.com 7 Alberto Pérez Veiga;
10 hagit berkovich; 18 Monkey Business Images

All other photographs are from:
Corel, digitalSTOCK, digitalvision, John Foxx, PhotoAlto,
PhotoDisc, PhotoEssentials, PhotoPro, Stockbyte

Every effort has been made to acknowledge the
source and copyright holder of each picture.
Miles Kelly Publishing apologises for any unintentional
errors or omissions.

Made with paper from a sustainable forest

www.mileskelly.net
info@mileskelly.net

www.factsforprojects.com

Self-publish your
children's book

buddingpress.co.uk

Contents

Why do cats lick their fur? 4
What do cats and kittens eat? 5
How does a cat show it's angry? 5

Why do kittens play? 6
How long do cats sleep? 7
What makes cats itch? 7

How do cats carry
their kittens? 8
Why do cats purr? 9
Are black cats witches' cats? 9

Can cats and dogs be friends? 10
Where did pet cats come from? 11
Why do cats eat grass? 11

What do kittens drink? 12

Are cats good climbers? 13

How long do cats live? 13

How fast do kittens grow? 14

How many toes do cats have? 15

Why do cats wear collars? 15

Are there wild cats in
the jungle? 16

Do all cats have long tails? 17

How many kittens are in
a litter? 17

Do cats visit the doctor? 18

Do cats like being picked up? 19

Why does a cat rub its head
on things? 19

How many kinds of cat
are there? 20

What does a cat's
meow mean? 21

What is the Cheshire cat? 21

What does a new cat need? 22

Do cats really have nine lives? 23

Are black cats really lucky? 23

How high can a cat jump? 24

Why do cats bring presents? 25

Are all cats furry? 25

Does a cat 'talk' with its tail? 26

How do cats keep their
claws sharp? 27

Do cats dream? 27

Why do cats love catnip? 28

How do cats hunt? 29

Which cat went to sea in a
pea-green boat? 29

Quiz time 30

Index 32

why do cats lick their fur?

Cats lick their fur to keep themselves clean. A cat's tongue has a rough surface, which helps to remove dirt, loose fur and small insect pests. A mother cat will lick her kittens to clean them and to bond with them.

Mother cat

Kitten

What do cats and kittens eat?

Cats are carnivores, which means they eat meat. Wild cats have to hunt other animals to eat. Pet cats and kittens eat special food made for cats, as well as meat and fish.

Kitten

Food bowl

COPY

Watch how your cat arches its back when it stretches. Can you can copy it?

HOW does a cat show it's angry?

An angry or frightened cat arches its back and makes its fur stand on end. This makes the cat look bigger than it really is and helps to warn off enemies.

Playtime!

When a cat plays with a toy mouse it's not just having fun, it is practising how to hunt a real one!

Why do kittens play?

Kittens play because it's fun! It's also good exercise and helps them to grow stronger. From four weeks old, kittens start to play. Play-fighting with their litter mates helps kittens learn how to get on with other animals.

Kittens playing with a ball of wool

How long do cats sleep?

Cats sleep for about 16 hours a day! Many cats rest during the day and are most active early in the morning and at night. Sleep is extra important for kittens because it helps them to grow.

Sleeping cats

Think
Work out how many hours you sleep at night. Do you have more or less sleep than a cat?

cats win!

Cats are the most popular pets. There are about eight million pet cats in the UK and six million pet dogs.

what makes cats itch?

A cat that keeps scratching itself might have fleas. These are tiny insects that live on animals. Fleas feed on an animal's blood, and their bite is very itchy. A cat with fleas should be seen by a vet.

Flea

How do cats carry their kittens?

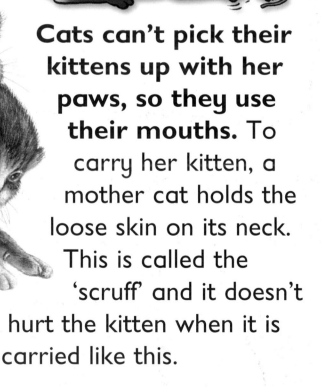

Cats can't pick their kittens up with her paws, so they use their mouths. To carry her kitten, a mother cat holds the loose skin on its neck. This is called the 'scruff' and it doesn't hurt the kitten when it is carried like this.

A mother cat carrying her kitten

Why do cats purr?

Cats usually purr when they are feeling happy and content. The noise comes from the breathing muscles in the cat's chest. If you put your hand on a loudly purring cat you can feel the vibrations of the sound.

Purring cat →

Speedy cat!

A pet cat can run at about 50 kilometres an hour. Cheetahs are the fastest wild cats and can run at twice this speed.

Are black cats witches' cats?

No, of course not! Many years ago some people believed that black cats were witches in disguise and that they helped witches to carry out their magic.

Purr

Practise making a purring sound. Relax your tongue, curl the end up a little and breathe out.

can cats and dogs be friends?

Yes, especially if they first meet when they are young. If a kitten and puppy grow up together they can get on very well. However an older dog may chase cats, and a cat will often hiss or swipe its claws at a dog.

Puppy

Kitten

Where did pet cats come from?

All pet cats probably came from a kind of cat called the wildcat. This cat still lives in the wild in Scotland, other parts of Europe, Africa and Asia. It looks like a pet tabby cat, but it is slightly larger.

Wildcat

Stick

Find pictures of cats in magazines and papers. Stick them on a piece of paper to make a collage.

Give me a home!

Lots of cats are made homeless by owners who don't want them any more. Rescue centres look after them and try to find the cats new homes.

Why do cats eat grass?

Eating grass helps a cat to cough up any loose fur that it has swallowed when cleaning itself. Grass also helps a cat to bring up bits of unwanted food, such as mouse bones and fur!

Fur ball

What do kittens drink?

Kittens drink their mother's milk for the first few weeks of their lives. A mother cat has teats, or nipples, on her tummy and her kittens suck on these to get milk. After four weeks, a kitten starts to drink water instead of milk.

Kittens suckling

Are cats good climbers?

Yes, cats are very good at climbing. They can scramble up anything that they can grip onto. Cats hang on with their sharp, strong claws and pull themselves up. Young cats sometimes have trouble getting back down again!

Cats climbing a tree →

clever cat!

Cats are very clever animals. They can even learn to open doors by pulling down handles with their paws.

How long do cats live?

Most pet cats live to between 12 and 15 years old. Some reach the age of 20 years old — that's nearly 100 in human years! One of the oldest cats ever lived to the age of 38.

Find out

Can you think of some other animals that are super climbers like cats?

13

How fast do kittens grow?

Kittens grow very quickly. They are born helpless – unable to see, hear or walk. By one week old their eyes open, and at four weeks they can run around. At eight weeks, kittens can eat solid food and are almost ready for life without their mother.

Newborn

One week old

Three weeks old

Four weeks old

Eight weeks old

Kitten's paw

HOW many toes do cats have?

Cats have 18 toes. They have five toes on each front paw and four toes on each back paw. Sometimes a kitten can be born with seven toes on one paw!

cat flap!

Many cats have their own special doors in and out of their owners' houses. Some can only be opened by a computer chip on the cat's collar.

Why do cats wear collars?

So that people know they have owners. A collar can carry a telephone number so that if the cat gets lost, it can be brought back home. Some collars also help to get rid of fleas.

make

Ask an adult to help you make a cat mask. Stick straws on a paper plate for whiskers, cut eyeholes and paint it.

Are there wild cats in the jungle?

A wild cat, called the jungle cat, lives in hot, wet forests in Asia. It hunts for rats, birds and fish along riverbanks and in swamps. Lots of other cats live in the wild, including big cats such as tigers.

Jungle cat

Do all cats have long tails?

No, they don't. There is a kind of cat called the Manx that does not have a tail at all. Another kind of cat called the Bobtail has only a very short stumpy tail – like a rabbit's tail.

Manx

Find out
Apart from tigers, can you name five other big cats? Use books and the Internet to help you.

How many kittens are in a litter?

Most mother cats give birth to four to six kittens at once – this is called a litter. Sometimes there can be as many as 12 kittens in a litter!

cat's eyes!
Cats have very good eyesight. They can see well at night – six times better than we can.

Do cats visit the doctor?

Yes, cats sometimes need to go to see an animal doctor called a vet. They are taken to the vet if they are ill, but also to have injections called vaccinations. These protect them from serious illnesses, such as 'cat flu'.

Vet examining a cat

Owner

Do cats like being picked up?

Some do, but some really don't. You should be careful when picking up a cat. Move slowly and calmly, and handle the cat gently. If it is not yours, check with the cat's owner first.

Lap lap!

A cat drinks by curling its tongue into a spoon shape and scooping up a little liquid at a time. It flicks water into its mouth and swallows every few laps.

Why does a cat rub its head on things?

To spread its scent. A cat will rub its head on its owner, or on furniture and other objects around its home. This marks out the cat's home area and warns other cats to stay away.

Play

Collect some sticks and pebbles and use them to mark out your own territory, or area, in your garden.

Cat rubbing its head against a chair

HOW many kinds of cat are there?

There are more than 100 different kinds, or breeds, of pet cat. Each breed has certain features, such as a particular fur colour and pattern, body shape or eye colour. Some breeds weigh twice as much as others!

Russian Blue

Longhair

Cornish Rex

What does a cat's meow mean?

Meowing is a cat's way of getting attention. A cat may meow to tell you it wants to be fed, stroked or let outside. A loud howl may mean a cat is in pain or upset. An owner quickly gets to understand the sounds their cat makes.

Claws out!

Cats have super-sharp claws. They are perfect for grabbing hold of wriggly prey, such as a mouse, during a chase.

Meowing kitten

What is the cheshire cat?

The Cheshire Cat is a character in the book *Alice in Wonderland*, written by Lewis Carroll. It is best known for its big smile. Alice sees the cat sitting in a tree. Then it slowly disappears, leaving just its wide grin, which vanishes last.

Create

Paint a picture of your own cat breed. Choose the colour and pattern you like and give your breed a name.

what does a new cat need?

It is a good idea to get a basic kit for your new pet. This should include bowls for water and food, cat food, and a litter (toilet) tray until the cat is old enough to go outside. Owners may also buy some toys, a brush and a bed for their pet.

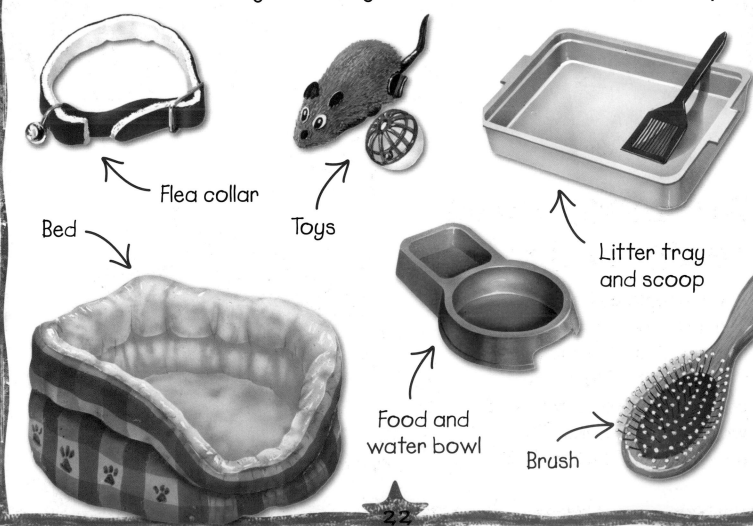

Flea collar

Toys

Litter tray and scoop

Bed

Food and water bowl

Brush

Do cats really have nine lives?

No, they don't. But sometimes it seems that cats can survive dangers that other animals can't. This is because a cat has excellent senses, strong muscles, good balance and super-fast reactions.

Tight squeeze!

A cat's whiskers are very sensitive. They help a cat judge whether its body will fit through a narrow space.

Black cat

Make

Scrunch up some paper and tie it on some string to make a toy for your cat to chase.

Are black cats really lucky?

Some people believe black cats are lucky, but others think they bring bad luck! Some people think that if a black cat crosses a person's path and walks away, it takes the person's good luck with it!

How high can a cat jump?

A cat can jump up to five times its height! Even a champion human high jumper can only jump a little higher than his or her own height. A cat's bendy body and the powerful muscles in its legs allow it to leap so far.

Cat jumping high in the air

Why do cats bring presents?

No one knows exactly why cats bring mice or other creatures to their owners. Mother cats bring prey for their kittens. Maybe cats bring gifts to show their owners that they think of them as part of their family.

Know that nose!

All cats have a pattern of ridges on their nose. Like a person's fingerprints, no two cats have exactly the same pattern.

Are all cats furry?

Most are, but there is one kind of hairless cat called the Sphynx. It looks like it doesn't have any fur at all, but it is covered in very fine fur, called downy hair, which is thicker on the tail and legs.

Sphynx

Does a cat 'talk' with its tail?

Yes, a cat uses its tail to send messages about how it is feeling. When a cat holds its tail straight up it is saying 'hello'. If it is sweeping its tail from side to side it may be about to pounce or attack.

measure

Gently, see if you can measure how long your cat's tail is using a tape measure.

Kitten holding its tail up

How do cats keep their claws sharp?

Cats keep their claws sharp by scratching. A cat will scratch most things, including furniture, so it is a good idea to buy a scratching post. Scratching removes old protective covers, called sheaths, from the claws.

Scratching post

Sniff!

A cat's sense of smell is about 14 times better than a human's – but not as good as a dog's!

Do cats dream?

Experts think that cats do dream. When a cat is asleep its paws and whiskers twitch sometimes. Scientists think that this is a sign a cat is dreaming, but they are not sure what they may be dreaming about!

Why do cats love catnip?

Catnip is a type of plant and it makes cats feel very excited! Many cats behave differently when they come near catnip — they rub themselves on the plant, roll around in it, lick it or eat it. Lots of cat toys contain catnip.

Cat eating catnip

HOW do cats hunt?

A cat creeps towards its prey very slowly. It moves quietly and crouches low to the ground to stay hidden. The cat gets as close as it can then makes a final speedy dash and pounces on its catch.

A cat hunting in the grass

Mouse

which cat went to sea in a pea-green boat?

The cat in the poem 'The Owl and the Pussycat', by Edward Lear. The author loved cats and drew many pictures of them. In the poem, the cat goes to sea with an owl.

puss in boots!

In the story *Puss in Boots*, written by Charles Perrault in 1697, a cat brings gifts to a king so his owner, a poor man, could meet and marry the king's daughter.

Quiz time

3. How long do cats sleep?

Do you remember what you have read about cats and kittens? Here are some questions to test your memory. The pictures will help you. If you get stuck, read the pages again.

page 7

1. How does a cat show it's angry?

page 5

2. Why do kittens play?

page 6

4. How do cats carry their kittens?

page 8

5. Are black cats witches' cats?

page 9

6. Can cats and dogs be friends?

page 10

7. Why do cats eat grass?

page 11

8. What do kittens drink?

page 12

9. Are cats good climbers?

page 13

10. Are there wild cats in the jungle?

page 16

11. Are all cats furry?

page 25

12. How do cats keep their claws sharp?

page 27

13. Which cat went to sea in a pea-green boat?

page 29

Answers

1. It arches its back and makes its fur stand on end to make itself look bigger
2. Because it's fun, and it helps kittens to grow strong and to get on with other animals
3. About 16 hours a day
4. They carry their kittens in their mouths
5. No, but some people once believed they were
6. Yes, if they grow up together
7. It helps them to cough up fur from grooming
8. Their mother's milk
9. Yes, they are expert climbers
10. Wild cats, called jungle cats, live in forests in Asia
11. Most are, but the Sphynx cat is hairless
12. By scratching
13. The cat in the poem 'The Owl and the Pussycat'

Index

A

Africa 11
Alice in Wonderland 21
Asia 11, 16

B

big cats 16
black cats 9, 23
Bobtail 17
breathing 9
breeds 20

C

cat flaps 15
cat flu 18
cat years 13
catnip 28
cheetahs 9
Cheshire Cat, the 21
claws 10, 13, 21, 27
climbing 13
collars 15, 22
Cornish Rex 20

D

dogs 10, 27
dreams 27

E

Europe 11
exercise 6
eyes 14, 17, 20

F

fleas 7, 15
food 5, 14, 22
fur 4, 5, 11, 20, 25
fur balls 11

G, H

grass 11
heads 19
hunting 5, 16, 29

I, J

insects 4, 7
jumping 24
jungle cats 16

L

legs 24, 25
litter trays 22
litters 6, 17
Longhair 20

M

Manx cats 17
meat 5
meowing 21
mice 5, 11, 21, 25
milk 12
mother cats 4, 8, 12, 17, 25
mouths 8, 19
muscles 9, 23, 24

N, O

noses 25
Owl and the Pussycat, The 29

P

patterns 20, 25
paws 8, 15, 27
pet cats 5, 7, 11, 13, 20, 22
playing 5, 6
purring 9
Puss in Boots 29

R

rescue centres 11
running 9
Russian Blue 20

S

scent 19
Scotland 11
scratching 27
scruff of the neck 8
sense of smell 27
sleep 7, 27
Sphynx 25

T

tails 17, 25, 26
tigers 16
toes 15
tongues 4, 9, 19
toys 9, 28

V

vaccinations 18
vets 7, 18

W

water 12, 19, 22
whiskers 22, 27
wild cats 5, 9, 16
wildcats 11
witches 9